MY FIRST PORTUGUESE BOOK

PORTUGUESE-ENGLISH BOOK
FOR BILINGUAL CHILDREN

 www.RaisingBilingualChildren.com

Alfabeto

A
o **avião**
airplane

B
o **barco**
boat

C
o **caderno**
notebook

G
a **garrafa**
bottle

H
o **helicóptero**
helicopter

I
o **iate**
yacht

N
o **nariz**
nose

O
os **óculos**
glasses

P
o **papagaio**
parrot

T
a **tartaruga**
turtle

U
o **umbigo**
belly button

V
a **vassoura**
broom

português

D
o **dedo**
finger

E
o **elefante**
elephant

F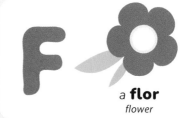
a **flor**
flower

J
a **janela**
window

L
o **livro**
book

M
a **mão**
hand

Q
o **queijo**
cheese

R
o **rato**
mouse

S
a **serpente**
snake

X
o **xilofone**
xylophone

Z
o **ziguezague**
zigzag

Animais selvagens | Wild animals

a **girafa**
giraffe

o **elefante**
elephant

a **zebra**
zebra

o **esquilo**
squirrel

o **veado**
deer

o **urso**
bear

o **leão**
lion

a **raposa**
fox

Animais domésticos

o **gato**
cat

o **rato**
mouse

o **galo**
rooster

o **coelho**
rabbit

o **cavalo**
horse

a **vaca**
cow

a **cabra**
goat

o **cão**
dog

o **pato**
duck

o **ganso**
goose

o **perú**
turkey

a **ovelha**
sheep

o **porco**
pig

Formas

o **círculo**

circle

o **quadrado**

square

o **triângulo**

triangle

o **retângulo**

rectangle

o **losango**

rhombus

o **oval**

oval

Shapes

o coração

heart

a estrela

star

a cruz

cross

a seta

arrow

o pentágono

pentagon

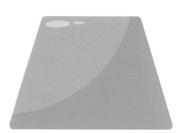

o trapézio

trapezoid

7

Frutos | Fruits

a **maçã**
apple

a **banana**
banana

o **ananás**
pineapple

o **alperce**
apricot

a **ameixa**
plum

a **pera**
pear

a **laranja**
orange

o **limão**
lemon

Bagas | Berries

o **morango**
strawberry

a **melancia**
watermelon

a **uva**
grape

a **cereja**
cherry

o **mirtilo**
blueberry

a **framboesa**
raspberry

o **kiwi**
kiwi

a **romã**
pomegranate

Vegetais

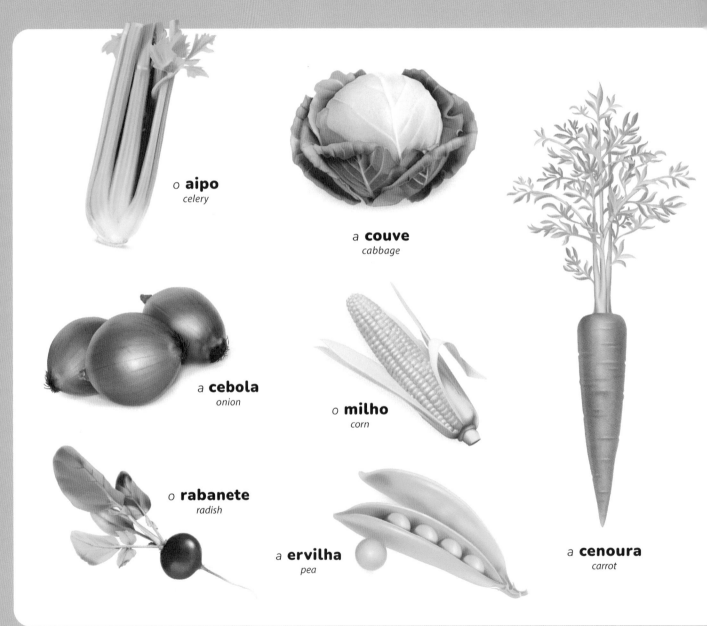

o **aipo**
celery

a **couve**
cabbage

a **cebola**
onion

o **milho**
corn

o **rabanete**
radish

a **ervilha**
pea

a **cenoura**
carrot

Vegetables

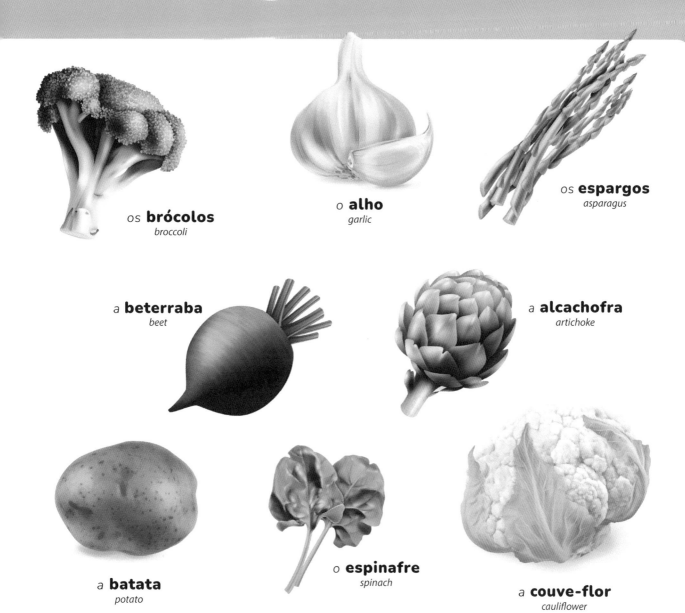

os **brócolos**
broccoli

o **alho**
garlic

os **espargos**
asparagus

a **beterraba**
beet

a **alcachofra**
artichoke

a **batata**
potato

o **espinafre**
spinach

a **couve-flor**
cauliflower

Números

um
one
1

dois
two
2

três
three
3

quatro
four
4

cinco
five
5

seis
six
6

Numbers

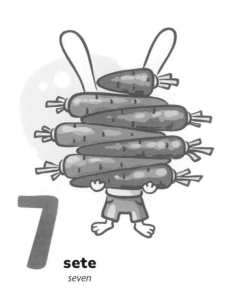

7
sete
seven

8
oito
eight

9
nove
nine

10
dez
ten

Cores

Vermelho *Red*

o **tomate**
tomato

a **joaninha**
ladybug

o **caranguejo**
crab

a **rosa**
rose

Amarelo *Yellow*

o **queijo**
cheese

a **abelha**
bee

o **trigo**
wheat

o **girassol**
sunflower

Colors

Verde *Green*

a **folha**
leaf

o **sapo**
frog

o **pepino**
cucumber

o **abacate**
avocado

Azul *Blue*

a **baleia**
whale

a **borboleta**
butterfly

as **calças de ganga**
jeans

o **peixe**
fish

Estações do ano

o **inverno**
winter

a **primavera**
spring

Seasons

o **verão**
summer

o **outono**
autumn

A minha casa

Cozinha *Kitchen*

o **prato**
plate

a **chávena**
cup

a **colher**
spoon

o **garfo**
fork

o **bule**
teapot

a **panela**
stock pot

Quarto infantil *Nursery*

o **berço**
crib

os **blocos**
blocks

a **boneca**
doll

os **anéis empilháveis**
stacking rings

My house

Casa de banho *Bathroom*

a **banheira**
bathtub

a **escova de dentes**
toothbrush

a **toalha**
towel

o **lavatório**
sink

Sala de estar *Living room*

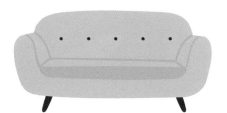

o **sofá**
couch

a **poltrona**
armchair

a **lâmpada**
lamp

a **televisão**
TV

Profissões

o **bombeiro**
firefighter

o **empresário**
businessman

a **médica**
doctor

o **cozinheiro**
cook

a **professora**
teacher

o **programador**
programmer

Professions

o **polícia**
policeman

a **astronauta**
astronaut

a **pintora**
artist

o **músico**
musician

o **jogador de futebol**
soccer player

o **agricultor**
farmer

21

Transportes

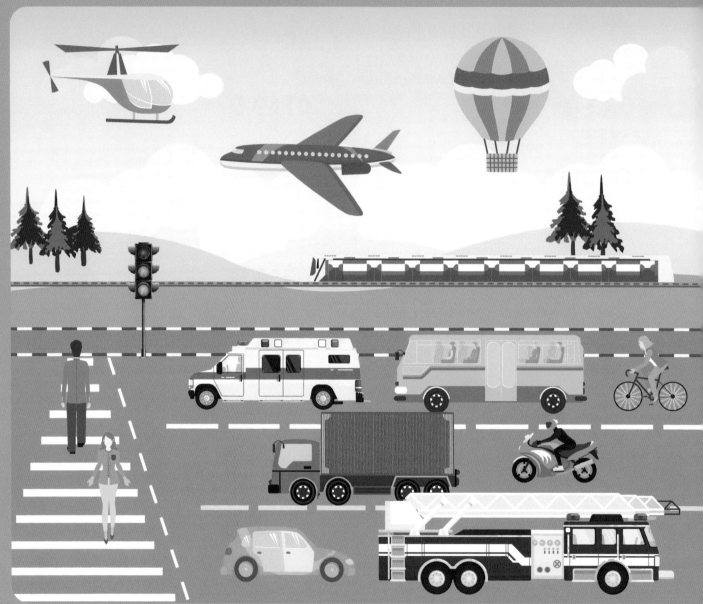

Transportation

o avião
airplane

o helicóptero
helicopter

o balão de ar quente
hot air balloon

o semáforo
traffic light

o carro
car

o camião
truck

a bicicleta
bike

a mota
motorcycle

o camião dos bombeiros
fire truck

o autocarro
bus

a ambulância
ambulance

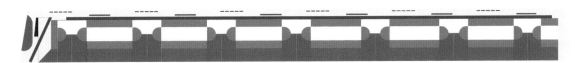

o comboio
train

Sons de animais

O GATO
MIA:
MIAU

O CÃO
LADRA:
AUAU

O SAPO
COAXA:
CROAC

O GALO
CANTA:
COCOROCOCÓ

O GANSO
GRASNA:
GÁ-GÁ

O PATO
GRASNA:
QUÁ-QUÁ

Animal sounds

A VACA
MUGE:
MUUUUU

O CAVALO
RELINCHA:
HINN-IN-IN

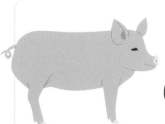

O PORCO
GRUNHE:
OINC-OINC

A CABRA
BALE:
BÉ-BÉ

O BURRO
ZURRA:
IHÓÓ-INHÓÓ

A ABELHA
ZUMBE:
ZZZZZZZ

Opostos

grande
big

pequeno
small

limpo
clean

sujo
dirty

quente
hot

frio
cold

o **dia**
day

a **noite**
night

Opposites

alto
tall

baixo
short

aberto
opened

fechado
closed

longo
long

curto
short

cheio
full

vazio
empty

PORTUGUESE-ENGLISH BILINGUAL BOOK SERIES

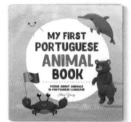

available on amazon

Questions?
Email us at hello@RaisingBilingualChildren.com

Printed in Great Britain
by Amazon

38629673R00018